Revealing Autism:

Discovering the voices of the masked.

By

Troy D. Walker.

Copyright © by Troy D. Walker 2022. All rights reserved.

Before this document is duplicated or reproduced in any manner, the publisher's consent must be gained. Therefore, the contents within can neither be stored electronically, transferred, nor kept in a database. Neither in Part nor full can the document be copied, scanned, faxed, or retained without approval from the publisher or creator.

Table of Content.

Introduction.

Autistic people, particularly adults, are more prone to using suppression and avoidance methods for anxiety and depression than other coping techniques such as seeking help or employing cognitive reappraisal. Suppression of unpleasant emotions can successfully mask the signs of depression, allowing the individual to "fly under the radar" and not receive the care they sorely require. Unfortunately, the unpleasant emotions do not go away; instead, they might exacerbate and prolong the melancholy phase and contribute to "depression episodes."

Many autistic people conceal their social communication challenges by employing observation, mimicry, intellectual analysis, and the usage of masks and personas, which can occasionally exacerbate these issues. We now know that while camouflaging is useful for handling daily tasks, it can also exacerbate mental health issues like anxiety and despair. The individual feels continually worn out, is susceptible to autistic burnout, and feels cut off from their true selves.

Some autistic individuals don't express their feelings in words, body language, or facial expressions. Autism affects the brain's circuitry, which controls how emotions are expressed vocally and physically.

Some of the obvious characteristics of autism due to this discrepancy include a facial expression that may be compared to a "wooden mask," reduced use of gestures, and a monotone speech tone. But if the individual does not seem or sound disturbed, there may be a failure to recognize their emotions, leading to further estrangement and sadness.

This may cause a depressive episode, and autistic individuals are far more likely to experience depression than non-autistic adults. Fortunately, depression may be treated after it has been identified.

Chapter 1.

What is Autism?

Autism, commonly known as an autism spectrum disorder, is a complicated neurodevelopmental condition that affects how children grow socially, intellectually, emotionally, and behaviorally, with males four times more likely to be affected than girls. Autism affects people with varying degrees of impairment. Autism is complicated to diagnose since some children with it only have moderate symptoms, while others must face more severe challenges.

What causes autism?

ASD's precise origin is uncertain. According to the most recent study, there is no one reason.

Some suggested risk factors for ASD include:

- Having an immediate family member who's autistic
- Certain genetic mutations
- Vulnerable X syndrome and other genetic diseases
- Being born to an elderly parent
- Low birth weight
- Metabolic disorder

- Maternal history of viral infection
- Fetal exposure to the drugs valproic acid or thalidomide.

Signs and Symptoms.

According to the fifth edition of the manual on mental disorders, often known as the DSM 5, some of the signs and symptoms that may suggest a child may have an autism spectrum disorder include issues with social communication and social interaction, challenges linked to confined repetitive patterns of behavior, and challenges with hobbies or activities. A child must also suffer a lot of difficulties in both of the following categories to satisfy the criteria for autism spectrum disorder. These issues must be apparent before early infancy and can cause damage to numerous aspects of the child's life.

Some instances of **social communication and social interaction issues** include;

- When you call a child's name, they may not turn around or look at you; they could have problems pointing or understanding facial expressions; they might also have issues establishing eye contact and seldom smile when they are grinned at.

- They don't express excitement when they solve a problem or win a game or don't engage in creative play, and by the time they are three years old, they may not even be speaking at all. They don't share their interests, experiences, or accomplishments with you.

Listed below is a possible timetable for this:

- **From birth:** problems keeping eye contact.
- **By nine months:** not reacting to their name.
- **By nine months:** not expressing facial expressions reflecting their emotions (such as surprise or rage) (like surprise or anger).
- **By twelve months:** not engaged in fundamental interactive games, including peek-a-boo or pat-a-cake.
- **By twelve months:** not employing (or just using a few) hand movements, such as hand-waving.
- **By fifteen months:** not sharing their interests with others (by displaying someone a favorite toy, for example) (by showing someone a favorite toy, for example).
- **By eighteen months:** not pointing or seeing where others point.
- **By two years:** not recognizing when others feel sad or hurt.

- **By two and a half years:** not engaged in "pretend play," including caring for a baby doll or playing with figurines.
- **By five years of age:** not playing turn-taking games, such as duck-duck-goose.

The following are some examples of **confined repetitive and sensory behavioral interests:**

• repetitive actions, including rocking, flailing their arms, twirling, or sprinting back and forth

• lining items, such as toys, up in tight order and feeling agitated when that order is violated

• Attachment to rigorous routines, including those surrounding sleep or arriving at school.

• repeatedly saying words or phrases that they hear others use.

• getting irritated over little changes.

• focusing attentively on pieces of items, such as the wheel of a toy vehicle or the hair of a doll.

• unusual responses to sensory input, such as noises, scents, and tastes.

• obsessive pursuits.

• exceptional qualities, including musical ability or memory capabilities.

Other attributes

Some autistic people could have different symptoms, including:

• delayed mobility, language, or cognitive skills

• seizures

• gastrointestinal issues, such as constipation or diarrhea

• excessive concern or tension

• unusual amounts of fear (either greater or lower than anticipated) (either higher or lower than expected)

• unanticipated emotional responses

• strange preferences or eating habits

• unusual sleeping habits

Another sign of autism is an **interest or preoccupation with certain things.** For instance, a kid with autism may get fixated on spitting the wheels of a toy truck rather than playing with it. Many kids with autism are also particularly sensitive to sensory events like bright lights, loud noises, or strong odors. Children may sit silently for lengthy amounts of time focused on certain things, like ceiling fans, or they may exhibit tremendous interest in activities, like flipping a light switch.

Remember that these are only a few instances of the symptom's children may exhibit; it's unlikely that another child would exhibit all of these traits in the same way.

They may also exhibit a constant lack of interest in or issues with the textures of foods or clothes, and for example, some kids cannot handle the feeling of garment tags or labels on their skin. In the first two years of life, if a kid exhibits just a few of these symptoms, it does not necessarily indicate they have autism. Some children may exhibit autism symptoms, but they ultimately outgrow them. On the other hand, rare autistic children may not truly exhibit these symptoms until much later in their childhood in some situations.

Chapter 2.

Autistic Masking.

Autistic masking, camouflaging, or compensating is a deliberate or unconscious suppression of inherent autistic behaviors. It involves concealing or regulating behaviors linked with autism spectrum disorder (ASD) that may be perceived as improper in settings. Autistic persons may feel the need to show or execute social behaviors that are deemed neurotypical or may conceal neurodiverse tendencies to be accepted and fit in.

An autistic person may masquerade to avoid being outed or harassed at school, work, or anyplace they may find themselves. It may make someone feel protected from misinterpretations or aggressiveness, but this act of self-preservation harms their self-worth and sense of self. Masking may lead to autistic burnout when life's problems strain a person's resources. Serious health issues, including despair and anxiety, might result from it.

Indications of Autistic Masking.

Depending on the person, masking, a social survival tactic, will seem different. Here are some indicators of disguising behavior:

- making unnatural or forced eye contact while conversing
- replicate grins and other facial gestures
- making gesture mimicry
- concealing or downplaying personal interests.
- building a repertoire of practiced replies to inquiries
- scripting talks
- enduring very uncomfortable sensory experiences, such as loud sounds
- concealing stimming habits (exchanging a favorite movement for one that is less noticeable or hiding a jiggling foot).

Reason for Masking?

The impulse to disguise might arise for a variety of reasons, such as:

1. Want to feel included and not stick out from the crowd.
2. Finding a job to satisfy work standards or increase employment possibilities.
3. One's worries for one's well-being and safety (bullying, verbal or emotional attacks, assault, intimidation).
4. To strengthen bonds and ties with other people.
5. To minimize the danger of failure in social settings by utilizing systematic approaches, so lowering uncertainty and improving confidence in the capacity to socialize.
6. To prevent prejudice and unfavorable reactions from others.

Negative impacts of masking.

Regular masking may have a tremendous influence on a person's well-being.

Some of the negative impacts of masking are:

1. Tiredness and fatigue: disguising requires a lot of work.
2. Alteration in how one views or identifies themselves (not feeling like one's actual self or like a "fake").
3. Elevated tension and anxiousness.
4. Depression.
5. Autism burnout.
6. A postponed diagnosis of autism.
7. Greater chance of lifelong suicidality and feeling like you don't belong.

Chapter 3.

Autistic Burnout.

Perhaps you've heard the phrase **"autistic burnout"** and are curious about what it means and how it came to be. Burnout, which is defined by tiredness in work life, is a phrase that is often used. The word "burnout" was first used by the autism community to describe all aspects of life. Autistic individuals had described instances when they were unable to manage, lost abilities, experienced loss of function, began behaving or feeling "more autistic" (increased repetitive behaviors or greater sensitivity to sensory input), lost work, performed badly in school, had relationship difficulties or suffered from mental and physical health concerns. These events may sometimes result in long-term impairment or suicidal ideation.

Only in the last five years have autism experts been aware of the burnout phenomena. Researchers have learned about it via online and in-person conversations with autistic persons.

Autistic burnout is a condition brought on by long-term stress and an imbalance between demands and capabilities in the absence of proper support. It is characterized by widespread, long-term (usually 3+ months) tiredness, loss of function, and diminished tolerance to stimulus.

It is commonly referred to as the acute physical, mental or emotional tiredness, frequently accompanied by a loss of abilities, that some individuals with autism suffer. Many autistic persons claim that the cumulative impact of navigating a world created for neurotypical people is the major cause of their condition. Burnout may notably impact autistic individuals with **good cognitive and linguistic skills and are employed or enrolling in school among neurotypical people.**

Why does autistic burnout occur?

When a person's capabilities are exhausted by life's trials, autistic burnout results, examples include:

1. A change in residence, the commencement of high school, the beginning of college, or old age.
2. When an autistic person uses scripted small chat, forces themselves to create eye contact, or hides repetitive actions, they are said to be masking or camouflaging.
3. Constantly adjusting to loud sounds is an example of sensory overstimulation.

4. Demands on executive function: juggling too many demands at once.
5. Stress, e.g., upheavals or turbulence in a person's life, such as losing a job or a relationship.
6. Lack of sleep, inadequate dietary intake, and dehydration.
7. Feeling less energized and requiring more leisure as we age.

What symptoms indicate autistic burnout?

The following are symptoms of autistic burnout;

• An absence of enthusiasm.

• Deterioration of executive function abilities (disorganized, trouble making decisions).

• Trouble caring for oneself (showering, personal hygiene).

• More readily prone to stress or breakdown.

• Selected mutism/loss of speech.

• Exhaustion or drowsiness.

• Physical ailments and intestinal problems.

• Memory deterioration.

• Absence of social skills or inability to conceal anymore.

• High energy levels might occur before the collapse.

• Behaving more autistically, such as by engaging in more repetitive actions.

What can an autistic person do if they are feeling burnt out?

The following are list of what one can do when having burnout.

1. Take a break and relax to allow your body to heal.
2. Make time for the pursuit of hobbies or interests that invigorate you.
3. Give yourself enough time to stop masking and suppressing stims.
4. Reduce demands and expectations. Let people know that what they are asking for is now too much.
5. Restrict your social contacts.
6. Exercise: Even a small amount of activity may assist in lowering anxiety and improving general well-being.

How can friends and family help?

As family and friend to an autistic person, we must understand that we also have a big role to play. Listed below are some ways we can be of help.

1. Do not demand that an individual alter or mask; accept them as they are.
2. Offer emotional assistance. Pay attention to what bothers them.
3. Provide direct help for everyday activities—assisting with cooking, food shopping, washing, etc.
4. Make adjustments at work, school, and in the community whenever necessary.
5. To lower the chance of burnout, emphasize autistic strengths and preservations.
6. Recognize that functional declines may indicate autistic exhaustion rather than inactivity or a lack of drive.

Note;

 The transitional age period, a period of significant change, is when many individuals describe experiencing their first autistic burnout. Due to the rise in expectations, the quantity and magnitude of life changes, and the overall stress of this developmental stage, entering adulthood is a sensitive moment. If a young person is experiencing autistic burnout for the first time, they may not comprehend what is happening.

Chapter 4.

Creating a Life for Autistics: Autism and Life Skills.

Independent living depends on daily skills, including personal cleanliness, food preparation, and money management. According to research, compared to their cognitive abilities, many people with autism spectrum conditions have difficulties with everyday life skills.

Acquiring basic skills is crucial for individuals with autism if they want to become more independent at home, school, and in their community. People with autism acquire the abilities that will enable them to boost their self-esteem and result in greater satisfaction in all spheres of their lives by introducing these talents early and building on them piece by piece.

What Do Life Skills Entail?

Life skills are also known as daily life skills or independent living skills. Basic living skills include taking care of oneself, cooking, managing money, shopping, organizing a space, and using transportation. These abilities are developed gradually throughout puberty and maturity, starting at home at a very early age.

It's crucial to acquire various life skills used in many different contexts. Additionally, it is crucial to teach executive function abilities, sometimes known as thinking skills, such as planning, organizing, setting priorities, and making decisions about each life skill being taught. Life skills may be categorized as follows:

- Safety and well-being
- profession and occupation
- Self-determination/advocacy
- peer interactions, socialization, and interpersonal communication
- Engagement in the community and personal finance
- Transportation
- Entertainment
- Homemaking abilities

How Can Life Skills Be Taught?

Since every person with autism is unique, the rate at which they are taught life skills will also vary from person to person. A young adult who has autism may eventually be able to live alone with little or no outside assistance, but another may need support and available services around the clock. Starting a child's life skill development as early as possible can benefit them later in life.

In addition to being taught and practiced at home, school, and community, many life skills need to be learned. Most autistic individuals gain from explicit, practical teaching in life skills that will boost their independence.

These abilities are often acquired via independent living courses or seminars taught by teachers or therapists. Training in life skills should occur in settings that closely resemble the circumstances in which the trainees will live and utilize their talents. This entails learning to cook in a kitchen or do laundry in a laundromat.

Ten Ways to Encourage Independence in Children.

1. Improve communication:

If a kid has difficulty speaking, improving communication skills and giving them the means to express preferences, needs, and emotions will be crucial in fostering independence.

2. Describe the Visual Schedule:

With the use of a visual timetable, you may assist your kid go more smoothly from one activity to the next. With your kid, go through each item on the timetable, and then tell them to double-check it before each transition. They will eventually be able to do this work more independently, gain experience in making decisions, and engage in the activities they find interesting.

3. Practice self-care techniques:

Self-care exercises should be included in your child's daily routine. Daily activities such as brushing one's teeth, combing one's hair, and other skills are important activities that should be taught to kids as soon as possible.

To help your kid get used to having them as part of the daily routine, incorporate these activities into his or her calendar.

4. Educate Your Child to Request a Break:

Ensure that your kid has the means to ask for a break by including a "Break" button on any communication devices they may be using, an image in their PECS book, etc. Determine a tranquil location where your kid can go if they're feeling stressed. Instead, think about providing headphones or other instruments to control sensory input. Understanding how to request a break may help your kid recover control over themselves and their surroundings, even if it may seem like a little thing.

5. Perform household duties:

Giving kids things to do may help them learn responsibility, include them in family activities, and provide them with valuable life skills they can apply as they age. You could think about doing a task analysis if you believe your youngster may have problems comprehending how to finish an entire assignment.

This technique entails breaking down challenging activities into manageable chunks. Make sure to act as a role model for your youngster or provide guidance if necessary.

6. Develop Your Money Skills:

The ability to manage money is a crucial one that may help your kid grow independent while out and about in the neighborhood. Whatever talents your kid now has, there are methods for him or her to start learning about money.

Consider including financial literacy in your kid's IEP at school, and when you are accompanying your child at a shop or supermarket, let him or her give the money to the cashier. You may instruct each stage of this method one at a time. Then, your youngster may start using these abilities in various community contexts.

7. Instruction on Community Safety:

Many families have serious safety concerns, particularly as kids become increasingly autonomous. Teach and practice travel safety lessons, such as reading signs and other crucial safety indicators and using public transit. Numerous helpful hints are included in the GET Going pocket handbook to assist people with autism in public transit. Consider letting your kid carry an ID card with his or her name, a succinct description of their disease, and a contact number.

8. Improve your leisure skills:

A kid will benefit from being able to participate in autonomous leisure and recreation throughout his or her life. It might be helpful to adapt particular interests in one or more topics that many people with autism have into age-appropriate leisure activities. Team sports, swim classes, martial arts, music groups, and other activities are included in the Autism Speaks Resource Guide for parents to engage their children in their local communities.

9. Instilling self-care in adolescents:

Teenagers with autism may experience many changes as they approach puberty and enter adolescence.

Therefore, it is crucial to teach them various hygiene and self-care skills. As they approach adulthood, your adolescents will be much more independent if you help them develop the habit of taking care of themselves. Your adolescent may benefit from visual assistance to complete his or her daily personal hygiene regimen.

To assist your teen in keeping track of what has to be done, consider creating an activity checklist and posting it in the bathroom. These may include taking a shower, cleaning your face, applying deodorant, and combing your hair. You may put together a hygiene "kit" to keep everything your adolescent needs in one place and remain organized.

10. Develop vocational skills:

As part of a personalized transition plan, your kid should have occupational skills included in his or her Individualized Educational Program (IEP) starting at age fourteen. Make a list of the child's abilities, passions, and talents and use it to inform the career-related activities included as goals. Take into account all the ways you have up to this point encouraged your child's independence: communication skills, self-care, hobbies and activities, and future objectives.

Chapter 5.

Cultivating a Neurodiverse World.

A person who thinks differently from the majority (neurotypical) is called a neurodivergent.

A person who thinks differently from the majority (neurotypical) is called a neurodivergent.

Around 4% of people have ADHD (attention deficit hyperactivity disorder), which may lead to impulsive behavior, concentration, and focus problems.

The following list of neurodiverse disorders should be familiar to society:

1. **Autism:** A condition that affects 1-2% of the population, autism alters how a person sees the world. Social engagement and development may be challenging and unsettling for those with autism.
2. **Dyslexia** is a disorder that makes people have difficulty understanding language, which may lead to problems with reading, writing, and spelling.

3. **Dyspraxia:** This condition hampers physical coordination and affects around 5% of the population. People may come out as awkward, disorganized, and unstructured.
4. **Dyscalculia** is a unique learning disability that affects the ability to acquire fundamental math facts, comprehend numbers, and carry out computations accurately and fluently.
5. **Dysgraphia**: a particular learning problem that impairs written expression. Dysgraphia may manifest as spelling errors, sloppy handwriting, and difficulty expressing ideas on paper.
6. **Tourette Syndrome** is a neurological condition that produces uncontrolled tics.

How to contribute.

People with neurological differences often experience mental health problems, such as stress, depression, and bullying. Make sure you contribute to creating a welcoming and caring atmosphere by enhancing well-being. Neurodivergent people will feel much safer and more confident if we have a good well-being system.

Encourage openness; for some neurodivergent people, it might be difficult to do so. Treating everyone justly makes it much simpler for them to discuss their differences and, as a result, much simpler to assist them.

Unity; We must be proactive and consider ways to include these individuals in every activity we participate in. This may be accomplished by participating in different awareness-raising events or simply setting an example by acting respectfully and equally.

Conclusion.

To better understand and appreciate those who are neurodiverse, the most important thing we can do is educate ourselves about autism. Nobody should have to alter who they are to satisfy someone else or a certain group. Our community today needs to know more about autism. Every educational program needs to include autism instruction. Due to our increased knowledge and understanding, people with autism will feel less stigma and pressure to fit in. Everyone should have access without having to "suck it up," as society expects.

www.ingramcontent.com/pod-product-compliance
Lightning Source LLC
Chambersburg PA
CBHW070732160726
48003CB00006BA/2470